LAYERS OF LEARNING

YEAR TWO • UNIT THREE

ISLAM
ARABIAN PENINSULA
CLOUDS & PRECIPITATION
CREATIVE KIDS

Published by HooDoo Publishing
United States of America
© 2014 Layers of Learning
Copies of maps or activities may be made for a particular family or classroom.
ISBN 978-1495295645

UNITS AT A GLANCE: TOPICS FOR ALL FOUR YEARS OF THE LAYERS OF LEARNING PROGRAM

1	History	Geography	Science	The Arts
1	Mesopotamia	Maps & Globes	Planets	Cave Paintings
2	Egypt	Map Keys	Stars	Egyptian Art
3	Europe	Global Grids	Earth & Moon	Crafts
4	Ancient Greece	Wonders	Satellites	Greek Art
5	Babylon	Mapping People	Humans in Space	Poetry
6	The Levant	Physical Earth	Laws of Motion	List Poems
7	Phoenicians	Oceans	Motion	Moral Stories
8	Assyrians	Deserts	Fluids	Rhythm
9	Persians	Arctic	Waves	Melody
10	Ancient China	Forests	Machines	Chinese Art
11	Early Japan	Mountains	States of Matter	Line & Shape
12	Arabia	Rivers & Lakes	Atoms	Color & Value
13	Ancient India	Grasslands	Elements	Texture & Form
14	Ancient Africa	Africa	Bonding	African Tales
15	First North Americans	North America	Salts	Creative Kids
16	Ancient South America	South America	Plants	South American Art
17	Celts	Europe	Flowering Plants	Jewelry
18	Roman Republic	Asia	Trees	Roman Art
19	Christianity	Australia & Oceania	Simple Plants	Instruments
20	Roman Empire	You Explore	Fungi	Composing Music

2	History	Geography	Science	The Arts
1	Byzantines	Turkey	Climate & Seasons	Byzantine Art
2	Barbarians	Ireland	Forecasting	Illumination
3	Islam	Arabian Peninsula	Clouds & Precipitation	Creative Kids
4	Vikings	Norway	Special Effects	Viking Art
5	Anglo Saxons	Britain	Wild Weather	King Arthur Tales
6	Charlemagne	France	Cells and DNA	Carolingian Art
7	Normans	Nigeria	Skeletons	Canterbury Tales
8	Feudal System	Germany	Muscles, Skin, & Cardiopulmonary	Gothic Art
9	Crusades	Balkans	Digestive & Senses	Religious Art
10	Burgundy, Venice, Spain	Switzerland	Nerves	Oil Paints
11	Wars of the Roses	Russia	Health	Minstrels & Plays
12	Eastern Europe	Hungary	Metals	Printmaking
13	African Kingdoms	Mali	Carbon Chem	Textiles
14	Asian Kingdoms	Southeast Asia	Non-metals	Vivid Language
15	Mongols	Caucasus	Gases	Fun With Poetry
16	Medieval China & Japan	China	Electricity	Asian Arts
17	Pacific Peoples	Micronesia	Circuits	Arts of the Islands
18	American Peoples	Canada	Technology	Indian Legends
19	The Renaissance	Italy	Magnetism	Renaissance Art I
20	Explorers	Caribbean Sea	Motors	Renaissance Art II

3	History	Geography	Science	The Arts
1	Age of Exploration	Argentina and Chile	Classification & Insects	Fairy Tales
2	The Ottoman Empire	Egypt and Libya	Reptiles & Amphibians	Poetry
3	Mogul Empire	Pakistan & Afghanistan	Fish	Mogul Arts
4	Reformation	Angola & Zambia	Birds	Reformation Art
5	Renaissance England	Tanzania & Kenya	Mammals & Primates	Shakespeare
6	Thirty Years' War	Spain	Sound	Baroque Music
7	The Dutch	Netherlands	Light & Optics	Baroque Art I
8	France	Indonesia	Bending Light	Baroque Art II
9	The Enlightenment	Korean Pen.	Color	Art Journaling
10	Russia & Prussia	Central Asia	History of Science	Watercolors
11	Conquistadors	Baltic States	Igneous Rocks	Creative Kids
12	Settlers	Peru & Bolivia	Sedimentary Rocks	Native American Art
13	13 Colonies	Central America	Metamorphic Rocks	Settler Sayings
14	Slave Trade	Brazil	Gems & Minerals	Colonial Art
15	The South Pacific	Australasia	Fossils	Principles of Art
16	The British in India	India	Chemical Reactions	Classical Music
17	Boston Tea Party	Japan	Reversible Reactions	Folk Music
18	Founding Fathers	Iran	Compounds & Solutions	Rococo
19	Declaring Independence	Samoa and Tonga	Oxidation & Reduction	Creative Crafts I
20	The American Revolution	South Africa	Acids & Bases	Creative Crafts II

4	History	Geography	Science	The Arts
1	American Government	USA	Heat & Temperature	Patriotic Music
2	Expanding Nation	Pacific States	Motors & Engines	Tall Tales
3	Industrial Revolution	U.S. Landscapes	Energy	Romantic Art I
4	Revolutions	Mountain West States	Energy Sources	Romantic Art II
5	Africa	U.S. Political Maps	Energy Conversion	Impressionism I
6	The West	Southwest States	Earth Structure	Impressionism II
7	Civil War	National Parks	Plate Tectonics	Post-Impressionism
8	World War I	Plains States	Earthquakes	Expressionism
9	Totalitarianism	U.S. Economics	Volcanoes	Abstract Art
10	Great Depression	Heartland States	Mountain Building	Kinds of Art
11	World War II	Symbols and Landmarks	Chemistry of Air & Water	War Art
12	Modern East Asia	The South States	Food Chemistry	Modern Art
13	India's Independence	People of America	Industry	Pop Art
14	Israel	Appalachian States	Chemistry of Farming	Modern Music
15	Cold War	U.S. Territories	Chemistry of Medicine	Free Verse
16	Vietnam War	Atlantic States	Food Chains	Photography
17	Latin America	New England States	Animal Groups	Latin American Art
18	Civil Rights	Home State Study	Instincts	Theater & Film
19	Technology	Home State Study II	Habitats	Architecture
20	Terrorism	America in Review	Conservation	Creative Kids

Unit 2-3 Printable Pack

This unit includes printables at the end. To make life easier for you we also created digital printable packs for each unit. To retrieve your printable pack for Unit 2-3, please visit

www.layers-of-learning.com/digital-printable-packs/

Put the printable pack in your shopping cart and use this coupon code:

2099UNIT2-3

Your printable pack will be free.

LAYERS OF LEARNING INTRODUCTION

This is part of a series of units in the Layers of Learning homeschool curriculum, including the subjects of history, geography, science, and the arts. Children from 1st through 12th can participate in the same curriculum at the same time – family school style.

The units are intended to be used in order as the basis of a complete curriculum (once you add in a systematic math, reading, and writing program). You begin with Year 1 Unit 1 no matter what ages your children are. Spend about 2 weeks on each unit. You pick and choose the activities within the unit that appeal to you and read the books from the book list that are available to you or find others on the same topic from your library. We highly recommend that you use the timeline in every history section as the backbone. Then flesh out your learning with reading and activities that highlight the topics you think are the most important.

Alternatively, you can use the units as activity ideas to supplement another curriculum in any order you wish. You can still use them with all ages of children at the same time.

When you've finished with Year One, move on to Year Two, Year Three, and Year Four. Then begin again with Year One and work your way through the years again. Now your children will be older, reading more involved books, and writing more in depth. When you have completed the sequence for the second time, you start again on it for the third and final time. If your student began with Layers of Learning in 1st grade and stayed with it all the way through she would go through the four year rotation three times, firmly cementing the information in her mind in ever increasing depth. At each level you should expect increasing amounts of outside reading and writing. High schoolers in particular should be reading extensively, and if possible, participating in discussion groups.

☺ ☺ ☺ These icons will guide you in spotting activities and books that are appropriate for the age of child you are working with. But if you think an activity is too juvenile or too difficult for your kids, adjust accordingly. The icons are not there as rules, just guides.

☺ GRADES 1-4
☺ GRADES 5-8
☺ GRADES 9-12

Within each unit we share:
- EXPLORATIONS, activities relating to the topic;
- EXPERIMENTS, usually associated with science topics;
- EXPEDITIONS, field trips;
- EXPLANATIONS, teacher helps or educational philosophies.

In the sidebars we also include Additional Layers, Famous Folks, Fabulous Facts, On the Web, and other extra related topics that can take you off on tangents, exploring the world and your interests with a bit more freedom. The curriculum will always be there to pull you back on track when you're ready.

You can learn more about how to use this curriculum at www.layers-of-learning.com/layers-of-learning-program/

UNIT THREE
Islam – Arabian Peninsula – Clouds & Precipitation – Creative Kids

The ink of the scholar is more sacred than the blood of the martyr.
-Mohammed

	LIBRARY LIST:
HISTORY	Search for: Mohammed, Islam ☺ Ayat Jamilah: A Treasury of Islamic Wisdom For Parents and Children by Sarah Conover and Freda Crane. ☺ Celebrating Ramadan by Diane Hoyt-Goldsmith. A look into one boy's experience of Ramadan with his family. ☺ The Great Night Journey by Anita Ganeri. A story from the Islamic tradition. ☺ The Hundredth Name by Shulamith Levey Oppenheim. Another tale from the Islamic world. ☺ I Am Muslim by Jessica Chalfonte. ☺ Islamic Stories by Anita Ganeri. ☺ Muhammad by Demi. Story of the man who started the Muslim world. ☺ The White Nights of Ramadan by Maha Addasi. ☺ The City by Katherine Hinds. A look at the history and development of Islam through the medieval period with beautiful illustrations. Also look for Countryside, Palace, and Faith by the same author for other aspects of Islam during the Middle Ages. ☺ Islam by Charles Clark. ☺ Islam from DK by Philip Wilkinson. ☺ Muhammad and Islam by Kerena Marchant. ☺ Muslim Festivals Throughout the Year by Anita Ganeri. ☺ Mosque by David Macaulay. Absolutely incredible drawings and a fictional, historically-based account of the building of a mosque. Worth buying if you can't find it in the library. ☺ Koran: Selections.
GEOGRAPHY	Search for: Arabian Peninsula, Saudi Arabia, Bahrain, Yemen, Qatar, Oman, etc. ☺ ☻ United Arab Emirates by Antonia D. Bryan. Part of the "True Books" series. Look for other countries in the region as well. ☻ ☻ Saudi Arabia (the World's Hot Spot) by Adrian Sinkler. Covers the religious and political forces that have made Saudi Arabia what it is. ☻ ☻ Tuttle Guide to the Middle East. Out of print. Covers each country and its formation and history since the fall of the Ottoman Empire. ☻ Arabian Sands by Wilfrid Thesinger. An Englishman travels among the Bedouin tribes of central Arabia. ☻ Arabia: Sand, Sea, Sky by Michael McKinnon. Strictly covers the natural world.

SCIENCE

Search for: clouds, precipitation, rain, snow, hail

😊 😊 😊 The Cloud Collector's Handbook by Gavin Pretor-Pinney. Makes cloud hunting fun.

😊 😊 😊 The Book of Clouds by John A. Day. Great photos of clouds and help in using them to forecast.

😊 Clouds by Anne Rockwell.

😊 Clouds by Marion Dane Bauer. An easy reader.

😊 Cloudy Day / Sunny Day by Donald Crews.

😊 It's Cloudy by Julie Richards. Extremely simple information for the youngest kids. Also look for It's Raining by Julie Richards. Part of the same series as It's Cloudy.

😊 Kipper's Book of Weather by Mick Inkpen. More fun than informational, but still a great way to begin a discussion of the weather for young kids.

😊 Rain by Marion Dane Bauer.

😊 Rain and Snow by Honor Head.

😊 Snow is Falling by Franklin M. Branley.

😊 The Story of Snow by Mark Cassino.

😊 The Cloud Book by Tomie DePaulo. Teaches the basics of clouds, mythology of clouds, and a little forecasting.

😊 Down Comes the Rain by Franklyn M. Branley.

😊 Weather Words and What They Mean by Gail Gibbons.

😊 😊 Eyewitness Weather DVD.

😊 Can It Really Rain Frogs?: The World's Strangest Weather Events by Spencer Christian.

😊 National Audubon Society First Field Guide: Weather by Jonathan Kahl.

😊 😊 The Secret Life of a Snowflake by Kenneth Libbrect.

😊 😊 The Man Who Named the Clouds by Julie Hanna and Joan Holub.

😊 😊 Peterson First Guide to Clouds and Weather by Jay Pasachoff and Vincent J. Schaefer.

😊 😊 Extraordinary Clouds by Richard Hamblyn. Weird and funky clouds.

😊 The Cloud Spotter's Guide by Gavin Pretor-Pinney. Funny and informative. You'll be forever looking up after reading this.

THE ARTS

Search for: cookbooks, art books, invention books, photography and cinematography books, other books that align with your specific creative interests.

History: Islam

Mohammed, having had visions, began to preach a new way to follow God in the year 610. He was run out of town for his pains. People most certainly did not want to hear it. After fleeing his home town of Mecca, he began to preach in Medina, where he had better success. But the people of Mecca, not content to let things lie, came and attacked Medina. Mohammad and his followers beat the attackers soundly, convincing many more people that God was indeed on their side. After that, Mohammed had excellent success preaching his new religion all over the Arabian world. His followers wrote down his teachings and the words given him by God in a book called the Koran (or Quran). Muslims believe it to be revelation straight from God, not at all corrupted by corruption or the distortion that comes with many translations over the years.

After Mohammed died, powerful leaders called caliphs spread his religion by the sword over more and more land. They butted into the Christians in Europe and the Buddhists in India and wars of religion became commonplace for the next millenia or so.

Mohammed is being given the Koran, revealed to him during a battle. Mohammed's face is not shown because Muslims believe that since the prophet is holy, he cannot be depicted.

Fabulous Fact

Muslims do not consider Mohammed to be the founder of their religion, but rather the restorer of the Adamic religion. Some say Mohammed was of the Hanif faith before his vision. The Hanifs were a monotheistic Arab religion that descended from Abraham. Mohammed claimed to be a direct descendant of Ishmael, Abraham's son by a concubine.

Over time Mohammed's followers split into groups just like the Christian church had split. The various groups of Muslims share many beliefs and all hold the Koran to be holy, but there are also many differences. Besides fighting against other religious traditions, they also fight among their own sects, just as Christians do.

☺ ☻ ☻ **EXPLORATION: Timeline of Islam**

There are printable timeline squares at the end of this unit.
- 610 AD Mohammed receives first vision
- 610-622 AD Mohammed preaches in Mecca
- 622 AD Hejira, when Mohammed flees Mecca (start of Islamic calendar)
- 630 AD Muslims capture Mecca, Arabian tribes vow allegiance
- 632 AD Mohammed dies and Abu Bakr is first Caliph
- 633 AD Muslim conquests begin
- 650 AD The Koran is written down for the first time
- 680 AD Shi'a sect begins
- 732 AD Muslim Empire reaches largest point

☺ ☻ **EXPLORATION: Hejira**

Mohammed was warned by his few followers that there was an assassination plot against his life in Mecca so he fled to the city of Yathrib, which was later renamed Madinat un-Nabib, meaning "city of the prophet." It was shortened to Medina later. This flight is called the Hejira.

Made a codex book of the Hejira. You will find a printable book at the end of this unit. Cut along the solid black line. Then tape the two pieces together to make a long strip. Color the pictures. Fold the book accordion style on the gray lines. Glue the backs of the pages together with a glue stick. Now read the story of the Hejira.

Fabulous Fact

The Hejira really divides Mohammed's life into two epochs. In the first half of his life he is an obscure trader who begins to preach and warn people, but is rejected. In the second part of his life he becomes a political leader who conquers the Arabian Peninsula by force and issues laws.

Additional Layer

The Muslim calendar begins at the Hejira, when Mohammed fled to Medina. It is based on a lunar calendar and does not compensate for the difference between the lunar cycle and the solar cycle so the months drift around the year. That is why Ramadan, the holy month of fasting, can fall at any time of year.

Famous Folks

When Mohammed was a teenager helping his uncle with the trading caravans, he met a Christian monk named Bahira who foretold Mohammed's future role as a prophet.

Additional Layer

Green is said to have been the prophet Mohammed's favorite color so you will often see it on flags of Islamic countries and in Islamic art.

Flag of Oman

Flag of Iran

Flag of Pakistan

Fabulous Fact

Whenever Muslims speak or write the names of the holy prophets they say "peace be upon him."

Additional Layer

About 3 million Muslims make the pilgrimage to Mecca each year and they all do it at more or less the same time, in the holy month of Dhu al-Hijjah.

☺ EXPLORATION: Constitution of Medina

For about 100 years before Mohammed was born the town of Yathrib (later renamed Medina) had been torn apart by blood feuds and conflicts between different tribes. There was a large Jewish population in the city, and they and one of the pagan Arab tribes had a long, ongoing dispute that seemed unresolvable without a third uninterested party to arbitrate. The people started to hear about this prophet fellow in Mecca and so they sent a delegation to ask him if he would come and solve their problems. At first Mohammed didn't, but when things got so bad that he had to flee Mecca, he went to Medina, where he knew he would be welcome. He set up a whole new law that codified the rights and responsibilities of all groups and members of the society. This law code became the basis of the Muslim Caliphates later.

The law code of Mohammed's day worked; it solved the disputes and united the tribes. Many of the tribes were soon converted to Islam, and Mohammed made sure they understood that their first duty was to their faith, even above the duty to their family or tribe. Mohammed used this unity and devotion to fight against and defeat, first Mecca, and then the whole of Arabia.

Jews, Christians, and other groups were given (mostly) equal rights under the law. While they were required to bear the cost of political wars of the community, they were not required to support the religious wars of the faith.

You can read it for yourself here:
http://www.constitution.org/cons/medina/con_medina.htm
It's not very long.

What do you think of the Constitution of Medina? How is it like modern constitutions? How is it different? The United States Constitution is based on the idea that there are two main principles, from Natural Law, that must be followed:
1. Do all you have agreed to do.
2. Do not harm others.

Do you think the Constitution of Medina is based on these principles? How can you tell?

☺ ☻ ☺ EXPEDITION: Mecca

Mecca was the city where Mohammed lived. Islamic people consider the city of Mecca to be the religious center of their faith and a holy city. They aspire to go there at least once during their lives.

You may not be able to jump on a flight to Mecca today, but you can see some of its sites anyway. Go to www.pbs.org/muhammed, then click on virtual Hajj. The Hajj is the pilgrimage Muslims make to Mecca. The site shows-and-tells about each step of the pilgrimage.

☺ ☻ ☻ EXPEDITION: A Mosque Near You

Make arrangements to visit a mosque near you. If you aren't Muslim they may not let you inside. Call first to see if you are welcome. Even if you can't go inside, a guided tour of the architecture of the outside of the building would be a great experience.

☺ ☻ EXPLORATION: Model Mosque

Muslim places of worship are called mosques and they are some of the most beautiful buildings in the world. There are many different architectural styles, but most mosques have a dome over the central place of worship, at least one minaret, a tall tower from which a man would call people to prayers, and only geometric designs. Representations of people or animals are forbidden in Islam so you won't find Muslim paintings like you would see in a Christian church.

Make a model mosque. Use a small square box for the base. Add a dome on top using an egg carton section that is cut out. Add minarets in the four corners using paper rolled into long thin cylinders. After you have it taped or glued together paint it out in light gray or brown, like the color of the stone used. You may also want to paint columns on the front and make the dome gold.

Additional Layer
The holiest city in Islam is Mecca and the holiest thing in Mecca is the Kaaba. The Kaaba is a square cube building built of granite. Inside there are verses from the Koran inscribed on the walls and an altar. In one corner of the building a stone had been set by the prophet Mohammed. It is an ancient stone venerated by Arab peoples since long before Muhammad and said to be descended from a sacred stone venerated by Adam and Eve. Muslims believe that it was Abraham who first built the Kaaba as a temple to God.

Additional Layer
"Mosque" just means place of worship. In a mosque, Muslims pray, learn from the Koran, and host dinners for their congregations, especially during Ramadan. Friday is the most important day of worship and prayers are always held in the mosque on this day. Mosques are also the places where Muslims bring their zakat, or charity, to be distributed to the poor. Sometimes schools, hospitals, libraries or gymnasiums are associated with mosques as well.

Explanation

Islam and Christianity and Islam and Hinduism became sworn enemies and still are, or at least the countries that are primarily Christian or primarily Hindu are antagonistic toward Muslim countries and vice versa.

In the very early days of Islam, Christians were already very negative about the new religion. It didn't help that the Arabs were a very warlike people who, when united in a group, made formidable and scary enemies.

Both Jews and Christians declared Mohammed to be a false prophet. One book, written in 634 AD, declares the Muslim invasions are the punishment of God against Christians. The Muslims by this time had already overrun Jerusalem and were preventing Christian pilgrims from entering the Holy Land. The book goes on to say the prophet Mohammed is "deceiving, for do prophets come with sword and chariot? . . . you will discover nothing true from the said prophet except human bloodshed."

Of course Muslims disagree.

☺ ☻ EXPLORATION: Mosque Mobile

At the end of this unit you will find an outline picture of a mosque. Make copies and glue it to a thin piece of cardboard, like a cereal box, and then cut around its outline. Color the mosque, and then add gold glitter to the dome. Use a hole punch to punch a hole in the top, and then hang your mosque up using a piece of yarn or string.

☺ ☻ ☻ EXPLORATION: Caliphate

After the Hejira, at Medina, Mohammed created a constitution establishing the rights and responsibilities of the people. After Mohammed's death his followers continued the government he set up. This became known as the caliphate. Caliph, meaning "successor." The Sunni sect believes the caliph should be chosen by election of the Muslim leaders, or nobility – in other words, an elected king. The Shiite sect believes the caliph should be a direct descendant of Muhammad which will indicate he was chosen by God – in other words, a hereditary kingship. It was this difference of opinion over the political succession that caused a split in the Muslim faith.

It was the Sunni elected leader who became the head of the caliphate in the years after Muhammad. The first hereditary period of the caliphate is known as the Rashidun. After the first few caliphs the Sunni established a hereditary caliph also, but not the direct descendant of Mohammad.

Color the map, which you will find at the end of this unit, showing the boundaries of the caliphates and the expansion of Islam over the world during the Middle Ages.

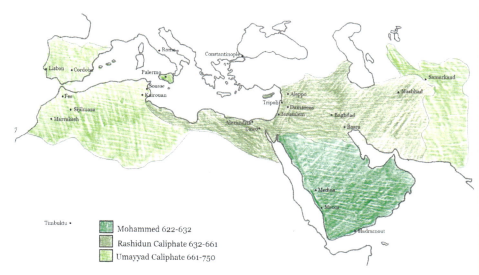

Fabulous Fact

The Muslim world as a whole is called the ummah, or community. It is an old word used by Mohammed to describe the new community of Muslims that he created, but before that the word indicated any community.

After 750 AD the caliphates begin to split and grow weaker, losing land, but many of the lands conquered remain Muslim, though not under the political power of the caliphate. In addition, caliphates were established in India and southeast Asia. There were many lands which adopted the Muslim faith, but were never part of any caliphate. Color another map, from the end of this unit, of the next thousand years of the Muslim world.

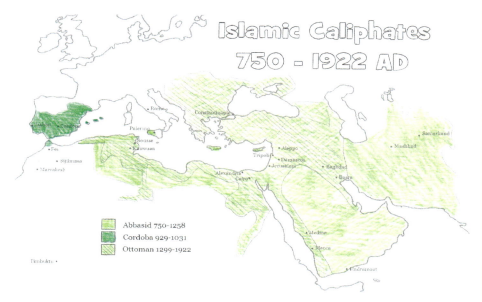

Additional Layer

No Muslim caliphate has existed since the Ottoman Empire lost power in the early 20th century, but many Muslims believe that it is an obligation for Muslims to unite under a caliphate, or in other words, under a political as well as religious empire. Some extremists also believe that it is the obligation of Islam to take over the world by force and establish Sharia Law so that there is an environment where Islam can flourish and all the people of the world can convert to it. Groups like Al-Qaeda and the Muslim Brotherhood exist in order to bring about this caliphate. But by far, the majority of Muslims want no such thing.

Now back up a moment and we'll insert the Fatimid Caliphate as well. The maps we've shown all give each of the caliphates at their greatest extent, but in between they were shrinking and growing, and so for part of that time there is another Islamic caliphate, this one Shi'a Muslim. It is called the Fatimid

Additional Layer

Mohammed's good friend, Abu Bakir, was elected the first caliph after Mohammed.

Additional Layer

The Abbasid Dynasty, together with the Cordoba Caliphate, are seen as the golden age of the Islamic world. Science, art, and literature flourished. There was peace, and trade and riches abounded.

The Abbasids emphasized scholarship and gathered wisdom from across the world including India, China, Greece, Egypt, Rome, Europe, North Africa, and the East Coast of Africa. They translated all that information into Arabic and later Europeans got hold of this wonderful knowledge and translated it into Latin, English, German, French and other European languages.

Calligraphy, miniatures, illuminated texts, philosophy, mathematics, trigonometry, and medicine were all preserved, studied and improved on by the Muslims.

The Thousand and One Nights was first collected and written down during this period.

Learn more about the Islamic Golden Age and the inventions and knowledge we owe to these people.

Caliphate because its rulers descended from Muhammad's daughter Fatima. The caliphate lasted until Saladin (the guy who fights Richard the Lionhearted in the Crusades) became sultan of Egypt and returned the caliphate to the rule of the Abbasids.

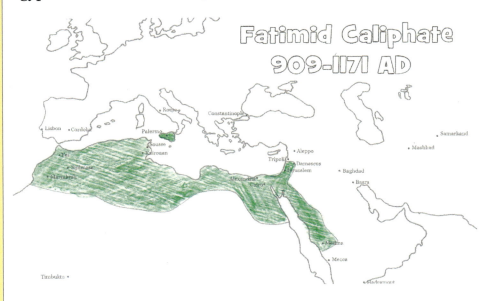

☺ 🟢 EXPLORATION: The Arabian Nights

The Arabian Nights, known in the Arab world as *The Thousand and One Nights* is a collection of stories written about a Muslim caliph in the late 700's AD. The caliph, according to the story, had a new woman brought to him every night and had her killed the next morning because he was so afraid she would be unfaithful to him (Ironic, isn't it?), but Scheherazade preserved her own life by telling the caliph a new tale each night for 1000 nights to keep him interested. She always ended the night with a cliff hanger.

The stories are a collection of many tales from India, Persia, the Middle East and North Africa. The were assembled little by little over time. Many of the tales have magic in them, but the real magic is a good story told in such a way that it keeps the attention of the audience.

Sinbad by Rene bull, published in an English version in 1898.

Set up a "tent" made of blankets, fill it with cushions and place some candles around. Then sit inside while you read one of the tales from the Arabian Nights to your kids. Introduce yourself as Scheherazade, use dramatic voices and make sure to stop at a climax of the story, even in the middle of a sentence. Keep your audience coming back night after night. Make sure to choose a good readable version in modern English.

Here is one good version: http://chestofbooks.com/fairy-tale/Arabian-Nights/index.html

☺ ☻ EXPLORATION: The Five Pillars
The five pillars of Islam are the five obligations a believer has to perform. They are:
1. Shahada: There is no God but God, Mohammed is the messenger of God. No criticism or deviance from this belief is allowed.
2. Salah: prayers five times a day, facing toward Mecca. These are ritual prayers with set movements and words.
3. Zakat: almsgiving. In most place the payment of zakat is voluntary, but expected. Zakat funds are given to the poor.
4. Ramadan: Muslims are expected to fast during daylight hours for the entire month of Ramadan.
5. Hajj: Pilgrimage to Mecca, at least once in a lifetime.

The Shiite Muslim sect has a little different take on the pillars, but basically it is the same across all Muslims.

Print the five pillars from the end of this unit. Cut out each rectangle and tape into a cylinder. You can print on green paper or print on white and decorate.

☺ ☻ ☻ EXPLORATION: Ibn Sina
Ibn Sina, also known as Avicenna, was a Persian mathematician and scientist who wrote some 450 documents on all sorts of

Famous Folks
Some of the caliphates were more liberal and tolerant of non-Muslims than others. The Fatimid and Abbasid caliphates allowed for the free exercise of minority religions in their realms.

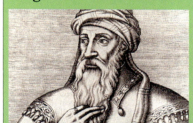

A prominent Jewish scholar, physician, and Rabbi of this period is Maimonedes.

Fabulous Fact
Just after Mohammed died, his successor, Abu Bakir, had to fight against rebel tribes and sultans in the Arabian Peninsula. These are called the Wars of Apostasy.

Additional Layer
Why do people fight over religion?

Isn't it interesting that religion, the thing that is supposed to bring people closer to God, is also the thing that is most often used as an excuse to kill our fellow man? Is it the way we worship God that is the real issue or is there some other aspect of human behavior that is the real problem?

subjects from medicine to astronomy, and from alchemy to theology to mathematics, and much more. He lived during the Islamic Golden Age of the Abbasid Caliphate.

Ibn Sina's Cannon of Medicine is his best known book (14 volumes actually) today. It was used as a medical textbook in Europe and the Islamic world until the 1600's and forms the basis of modern medicine. A lot of it was completely wrong, but Ibn Sina did correctly diagnose and describe diseases and body functions that wouldn't be rediscovered in Europe for another 400 years or so.

Make a tin can punched lantern to represent the light that is spread through knowledge. Just save and clean a 'tin" can and then fill it with water and freeze it. The ice will keep your can from getting dented as you hammer holes in the can. Create a dot design on paper. Then wrap the paper around the can and punch holes at each point on your design. Place a votive candle in the bottom of the can.

☺ EXPLORATION: The Hundredth Name

Muslims believe there are 100 names for God. They call him Allah. They believe we know 99 of his names, but that the hundredth name is a mystery that we can't know. If we did know the final name, we would be given an eternity in paradise.

There is an ancient riddle that asks, "Why does the camel smile? Because he knows the hundredth name of God." Some Christians believe they know the hundredth name, and that it is Abba, or

Father. In other words, they believe that anyone can know the name, but it is the relationship with God that will grant them paradise.

Read *The Hundredth Name* by Shulamith Levey Oppenheim from the library list. It is a picture book about this story and belief.

☻ ☻ EXPLORATION: Mohammed's Meals

Mohammed taught many things to his followers; one of those teachings was the principle of fasting. All during the month of Ramadan, Muslims fast during the daylight hours. Fasting is going without food or drink.

Do you think you could fast for a whole day? Try it. From the time you wake up, until nightfall, don't take any food or water. It's very difficult. Doing this all the time could be harmful to your health, but one day won't hurt you (though your stomach will growl!). Muslims fast during the day for 29 or 30 days all throughout Ramadan. It teaches them patience, humility, and to be more spiritual and rely on Allah (God).

☻ ☻ ☻ EXPLORATION: Prayer

Mohammed taught Muslims to pray five times per day. Talk with your family about prayer. Consider whether or not you pray and why. Why do you think virtually all religious leaders encourage prayer? What does the practice do for people?

Make a prayer rug. Islamic people lay a special rug down on the floor, facing the Holy City of Mecca, and kneel on it and sit on it during their prayers. It isn't just a piece of fabric; it is a holy object and is shown respect.

Additional Layer

Muslims do not believe in the concept of "vicarious atonement" but rather believe in the law of personal responsibility. Islam teaches that each person is responsible for his or her own actions. On the Day of Judgment Muslims believe that every person will be resurrected and will have to answer to God for their every word, thought, and deed. Consequently, a practicing Muslim is always striving to be righteous.

Additional Layer

Green has long been a color that represented Islam, but other colors in the Islamic world have significance as well.

White is a symbol of purity. Black is a symbol of modesty, which is why many women wear a black cloak or robe.

In Shi'a countries only men who are descended directly from the Fatimid line are allowed to wear black turbans.

You'll need:
- a piece of fabric 24" x 16" for each child. Choose a solid color.
- Wide ribbon, at least ½ inch or wider
- fringe, 32"
- fabric glue
- fabric paint or markers

1. Fold the raw edges of the fabric over and use the glue to secure.
2. Glue the ribbon all around the border of the fabric.
3. Glue the fringe on to the two short ends of the fabric.
4. Decorate the center of the rug in any designs you like.

☺ ☻ ☻ EXPLORATION: Symbol of Islam

The crescent moon and star together are the symbol of Islam. It represents Islam guiding its followers just like the moon and stars guided travelers.

Using construction paper, scissors, and glue, or other craft supplies, create your own version of the Islamic crescent moon and star. It is seen in many styles and colors, so be creative and make one that suits you.

GEOGRAPHY: ARABIAN PENINSULA

The Arabian Peninsula is mostly desert, the interior portion so dry and barren that it is called the Rub al Khali, or the Empty Quarter. For thousands of years desert tribes have wandered from oasis to oasis following the sparse grasses and water with their herds of goats, sheep, and cattle. The coastal regions are more fertile and support more permanent cities; that's where organized countries with firm borders were even back into ancient times.

The land is criss-crossed with Wadis, or seasonal streams. There are large underground aquifers that are the source of the oases, some large enough to support farmland. The Arabian Peninsula includes the modern countries of Saudi Arabia, Yemen, Qatar, Oman, Bahrain, Kuwait, and the United Arab Emirates. Their governments are a product of the ancient Arab traditions, Islamic traditions, and European colonialism.

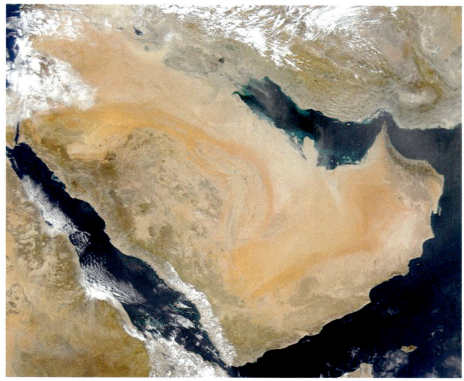

Bahrain is a constitutional monarchy, which means the king is constrained by the law and there is a parliament which helps to govern the country. In addition, Bahrain recognizes the right of women to vote and be educated. Bahrain is the economic capital of the Middle East, not surprising since it has the freest markets in the region.

Additional Layer

Looking at a map of the peninsula, it is obvious to see that it lies on its own tectonic plate.

Teaching Tip

There's a lot about the Middle East that isn't pretty. There are really great and wonderful things too. Share both with your kids at age appropriate levels. Places, events, cultures, attitudes, customs, and governments, good and bad, need to be examined so we can learn to embrace the good and recognize and reject the bad.

Additional Layer

The United States was the first country to have a written constitution which restricted government. (Other countries have had constitutions that guaranteed certain rights to people). The United States also successfully showed the power of a free market. Many of the countries of Arabia have followed this example. Are they better for it or worse? What effect does freedom have on a people?

Fabulous Fact

Massive dust storms can blanket vast regions of the desert.

Additional Layer

What difference do you think having a free press makes to a nation? Why do people want to censor or restrict the press?

What is the responsibility of the press?

Additional Layer

Review the geographic concepts of oasis, desert, peninsula, and archipelago.

Additional Layer

In what may seem to be a counter intuitive turn of events, the Saudi government has purposely destroyed hundreds of historic buildings including those dating back to Mohammed and his immediate family members.

The Saudi brand of Islam fears idolatry and the possibility that a place or object could come to be worshiped.

Kuwait is also a constitutional monarchy, having been heavily influenced by the British, as was Bahrain. As such, it has a greater degree of freedom and wealth than many other Arab nations. Kuwait has massive environmental problems as a result of the Iraqi invasion of 1991 when the retreating Iraqi army set fire to Kuwait's oil fields, wreaking havoc and causing massive spills and soil contamination.

Oman is ruled by a hereditary sultan with an elected advisory council. All citizens over the age of 21 can vote for the advisers. Oman has only very recently begun to make progress in the areas of education and industry, but their government is embracing more and more free market principles in the hope of bringing growth and independence to the nation. It does not have oil reserves sufficient to support massive booms like Kuwait and Bahrain experienced. The government is by far the largest employer in the nation.

Qatar is another oil boom nation. It is an absolute monarchy, but has a constitution and many freedoms for its people, including the women who live there. Over time they have tended to more and more free markets. Qatar is the base of the Arab news channel Al Jazeera, which is highly controversial in many countries as the only editorial Arab news channel.

The United Arab Emirates is a federation of seven independent states as the United States is a federation of states. It is a constitutional monarchy, with a federal division of powers where each of the seven states is an absolute monarchy, but governed from a federal central presidential power. Confused yet? It is similar in structure to the United States, but in practice many offices are hereditary and the nation has much less freedom, though more than Saudi Arabia, for example. The nation is oil-rich and that is aiding its development dramatically. The official state religion is Islam, but people of other faiths are unmolested as long as they do not attempt to proselytize.

A town in Yemen

Yemen is a republic plagued with corruption, which prevents

the country from making much headway economically or socially. Their oil reserves are small, but they are heavily dependent on them for their government revenues. The country is seriously struggling under inadequate education and insufficient economic resources.

Saudi Arabia, covering most of the land mass of the peninsula, is an absolute monarchy. They claim the Qur'an as the constitution of their state and use Sharia Law in their courts. Sharia Law is based on Islamic teachings and has extremely harsh punishments, strict rules, and demotes women to a subservient class with few rights. Religions other than Islam are illegal in Saudi Arabia. They have a public education system which teaches primarily the Islamic religion and little else. Their economy is based almost solely on oil.

Muslim pilgrim at Mecca. Below you see a vast crowd of worshipers. Photo by Ali Mansuri and shared under CC license.

The people of the Arabian Peninsula are overwhelmingly Muslim and the center of Muslim religion is found at Mecca in Saudi Arabia. The area has vast oil reserves that were developed through western funding and have served to make these countries wealthy as political units, though many of their people suffer in poverty. Other economic activity includes growing of dates and exotic fruits and spices. The Arabic language is the official language in most countries, though English is widely spoken by the more educated, especially in the larger cities.

Additional Layer

OPEC, Organization of Oil Exporting Countries, several of which are on the Arabian Peninsula, has had a huge effect on worldwide oil prices for decades.

Famous Folks

Sheikh Khalifa bin Zayed al-Nahayan is the president of the United Arab Emirates and the emir of Abu Dhabi. He is fabulously rich with about US $19 billion in assets. He has given large grants to Johns Hopkins Medical Center where a new cardiovascular tower is to be named after him. He also is a large donor to a university in Wales, supports an education fund, and gives heavily to cancer research.

Fabulous Fact

The Dubai Shopping Festival is a month long celebration of commerce. Stores have really great deals and coupons.

There are fireworks every night and events from around the world. Each part of the world gets its own section of the festival and food. Wares from around the globe are sold and celebrated.

Dubai, UAE

Additional Layer

Child marriage is a problem in many parts of the Arabian Peninsula with some girls as young as nine being forced to marry men decades older than they.

This tradition stems back to tribal law and practices from ancient times, not from Islam.

On The Web

Read this great explanation of how oil drilling works and watch a clip from "Dirty Jobs" on an oil rig.

http://science.howstuffworks.com/environmental/energy/oil-drilling.htm

☺ ☺ ☻ EXPLORATION: Arabian Peninsula Map

Make a map of the Arabian Peninsula. Use the printable map from the end of this unit. Look back at the satellite map of the Arabian Peninsula from the start of this section. What is the terrain like? Now look at Arabia in your student atlas. Can you find oil wells, oases, major cities, and the seas?

Show these things on the map:
- Location of major oil wells
- Other economic resources
- Country borders, capital cities, other major cities
- Seas surrounding the peninsula.

After you have labeled and colored your map, mount it on cardboard, like from a cereal box, and cut apart the countries to make a puzzle. Put it together a few times.

☺ ☺ ☻ EXPLORATION: Oil Boom

The Saudi Arabian oil fields were first drilled in 1946 by American companies, Standard Oil (later Exxon) and Socony-Vacuum (later Mobile). Oil exploration by American and British companies continues to today. The oil discovered has made the countries rich in oil and rich in everything else. In most cases not much of that ever reaches the people. Part of the problem is that oil is the only industry in Saudi Arabia, and so even though it makes a lot of money through worldwide sales (especially to Americans), it provides relatively few jobs.

Countries like Saudi Arabia are actively working to create new industrial parks and cities in order to diversify their economies, and the oil money makes the prospect hopeful, though hampered by a controlling government structure and royal families that like their luxuries.

In the 1960's and 70's, because of the oil boom, Kuwait went from being an antiquated, obscure, and achingly poor country to a modern city of skyscrapers and financial centers with the eighth highest per capita income in the world and the world's strongest currency. Of course, this sort of behavior makes the neighbors jealous and Iraq invaded in a bid to take over the oil fields in 1990, sparking a counter-war led by the United States.

Get a tall container, like a juice pitcher. Fill it ½ full of water. The water represents oil trapped below the surface of the earth. Now get a large sheet of plastic wrap and carefully lay it on top of the water and slowly pour sand over the plastic wrap. The plastic wrap and sand should press down on the surface of the water, but not go below. Now take a straw and forcefully poke it through the sand and plastic wrap into the water. Water will come spurting out of the straw. This is what happens to oil under the surface of the earth. As soon as a pocket is drilled into it wants to come shooting out because under the earth it is under pressure.

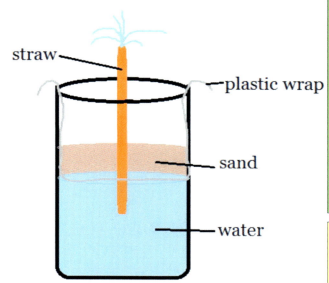

EXPLORATION: Bahrain

Bahrain is an archipelago and is surrounded by both salty and freshwater seas. How can this be? There are freshwater springs in the ocean and part of the water is not yet mixed with the salt.

Want to see why this happens? Gather these supplies: 3 glasses, blue food coloring, water, salt, and 3 eggs.

Sharia

Sharia Law is based on the Koran and the teachings and life of the prophet Mohammed. It is not based on codified law or on judicial precedent. Each case stands alone and each judge is free to rule as he sees fit without regard to previous decisions made by himself or other judges. No one can can therefore fully know the law or the probable consequences of breaking it before he is judged by one individual who is not accountable to the people.

The specific way Sharia is implemented is highly dependent on the brand of Islam being practiced and the cultural norms of the society it is practiced in. So countries relying on Sharia Law can have very different human rights records and levels of freedom and justice. Saudi Arabia, a sharia state, has been criticized as one of the worst offenders in the world.

In Saudi Arabia secret trials, torture, beheadings, amputations, stonings, lashings for minor crimes, and other brutal practices are the norm. Often the accused doesn't even know which crime he is being tried for.

Fill the first glass with water, then add several drops of food coloring. Drop the egg in – it will sink because the egg is more dense than the water.

Fill the second glass with warm water, then add 6 tablespoons of salt and several drops of food coloring. Mix well. Drop an egg in and it will float. The egg is less dense than the saltwater.

In the third glass, fill it about 2/3rds full of warm saltwater. Then slowly and carefully pour water that is dyed blue on top. Drop the egg in and watch it float between the two layers of water.

The differing densities of water create a barrier. This is the same thing happening in the freshwater springs of Bahrain. The freshwater, less dense than the surrounding saltwater, stays separate for a time. It will eventually mix, but since there is a continual spring, there is a continual pocket of fresh water there.

☺ EXPLORATION: Watch Out, They Spit

Camels are really important to the people of Arabia. Learn more about camels and then do this craft to make your own camel.

1. Glue two large brown or tan or yellow (or pink, whatever!) pompoms together.
2. Add legs made from felt.
3. Glue on a head with a smaller pompom.
4. Add ears of felt, a felt tail, and googly eyes to finish it off.

☺ ☺ ☺ **EXPLORATION: Make a flag bunting.**

Use construction paper, markers, crayons and so on to make a string of small, quarter sheet size flags, one for each country. Tape or glue the flags together along a string or piece of yarn to make a bunting you can hang on your wall.

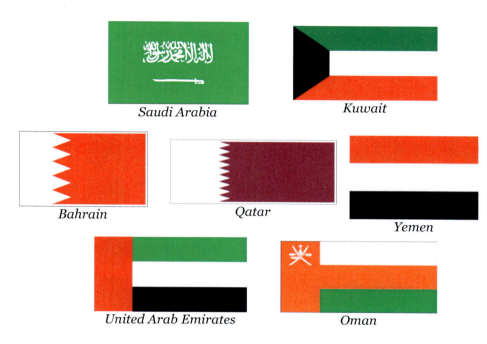

Saudi Arabia

Kuwait

Bahrain

Qatar

Yemen

United Arab Emirates

Oman

Research one of the flags to find out what the colors and symbols mean.

☺ ☺ **EXPLORATION: Argh, Matey**

The states of the United Arab Emirates used to be known as the Pirate Coast. Make an old fashioned Arab pirate ship model. The ships used in the Red Sea, Indian Ocean, and Gulf were called Dhows and had one or more triangular lateen sails. They were used for trade as well as pirating. Many sailing dhows still sail the ancient trade routes to India and Africa and are used as fishing vessels.

1. Make the hull of the ship from a cardboard box.
2. Cut the front of the box into a triangle and curve the sides in and tape in place. (A milk carton is already the right shape.)

Additional Layer

Camel spiders went viral in the west after American troops sent photos of the large creatures home. They run fast, seek shade (which can make you think they're chasing you when really they want your shade), jump on the bellies of camels, and suck the camels' blood. They live in the deserts of Arabia and other parts of the Middle East.

Camel spider fighting a scorpion

Famous Folks

Tawakel Karman is a Nobel Peace Prize winning journalist and advocate for women's rights and freedom of the press in Yemen.

Learn more about her.

Additional Layer

The Arabian Oryx is a type of antelope.

It lives in the deserts and the steppes and nearly went extinct, but was saved and bred by zoos in the 1970's and reestablished in the wild where it remains vulnerable.

3. Paint the box with brown paint (spray paint is nice and easy and dries quickly).
4. Punch two holes through the top "deck" of the box, just large enough for a straw to fit through and secure with tape or hot glue.
5. Cut a piece of paper into a triangular sail.
6. Tape your triangular sails to two straws (cut to 2/3 the length of your mast) and attach the straws to the tall masts at an angle with hot glue. Use string and tape to secure the lower corner of the sails to the deck or use a dot of hot glue.

😊 😊 😊 **EXPLORATION: Flat Bread**

In Saudi Arabia, like the rest of the Middle East, the cuisine has been greatly influenced by Turkey, Persia, and Africa. Flat bread is served with nearly every meal. Here is how to make it:

Preheat the oven to 450 degrees F. In a large mixing bowl combine:
     1 ¼ cups very warm, but not boiling, water
     2 Tbsp. yeast
     2 Tbsp. of margarine or shortening

Stir briefly, then let it sit for about five minutes. Then stir in 1 ¼ cups of flour with a hand mixer. Add another cup of flour and mix. Then add flour ¼ cup at a time until you can add no more flour. Turn the dough out onto a counter and knead in as much flour as you can. Divide the dough into 12 equal pieces and form each piece into a very smooth ball. Cover the dough balls with a clean towel and let it sit for ten minutes.

Gently flatten one dough ball at a time with your fingers. Then roll into a flat circle with a rolling pin, being careful to work from the center outwards and not crease or tear the dough.

Place two dough circles onto an ungreased cookie sheet and bake for 3 minuets at 350 degrees F. Turn over and bake for two more minutes. Then roll out your next two dough circles and bake them, continuing until all the dough is baked.

Additional Layer

The Lanner Falcon lives in the Arabian Peninsula, Africa, and southeast Europe and hunts smaller birds.

Besides flat bread, fresh fruit and dates are also served with nearly every meal. See if you can find some dates to try.

Deep Thoughts

Oil transformed the Middle East in the 1960's and 70's. Today the Middle East is being transformed by Facebook.

The internet, a globally connected world, and instant messaging are changing how people get their information, their degree of dependency on government, and how people organize and connect with one another.

What changes have you seen in the world due to new technology?

I Want That Tax Structure!

Bahrain has no personal income taxes, no wealth taxes, no inheritance taxes, no capital gains taxes, and no sales tax.

They do tax property when it passes hands, not every year. Oil companies (and no others) are taxed at a 46% flat rate.

Additional Layer

This huge mall, called *The Avenues*, could be found in any major western city. It is in Kuwait where some of the women and men still dress in traditional Arab dress, but most dress like westerners, including nearly all the younger generation.

Are they losing something or gaining it? Which traditions should a culture hang on to and which should go? And should those things be controlled by governments or not?

Photo by Steve and Jem Copley and shared under CC license.

😊 😊 😊 EXPLORATION: Mud-Brick Skyscrapers

The city of Sibam in Yemen is built of mud bricks in tall buildings between five and eleven stories high. The unusual thing is that they have been built this way since around the 300's AD. The residents built the tall buildings to help ward off and defend against Bedouin attacks. Notice that there are no windows on the ground floor and on subsequently higher floors the windows grow larger as you near the top of the building.

The skyscraper city of Sibam, Yemen.
Photo by Jialiang Gao and shared under CC license.

Make a clay model of one of the buildings or of the whole town. Notice the wall around the town. Remember the buildings are made of mud brick and therefore melt in the rain. They have to be constantly maintained and rebuilt to keep them in good repair.

Check to see if your library has *Architecture of Mud*, a documentary film produced in 1999 about the town.

😊 😊 EXPLORATION: How to Tie a Turban

You'll need a piece of fabric about 16 to 16 ½ feet long. We recommend you use an old sheet, cut the long way into 1 foot wide strips and fastened end to end. Then watch this video to make your own turban.
http://www.dailymotion.com/video/xgf0dy_how-to-tie-a-turban_lifestyle

😊 😊 😊 EXPLORATION: Bedouin Dance

This video of Bedouin dance: http://youtu.be/pldqku1iO8A was actually shot in Syria, but the dance is similar across the Arab world. Notice the strong repetitive beat, the energetic music, and the energetic movements. Also notice that the dancers are all men and always have been all men. Look for other examples of Bedouin dance.

Most Bedouin dance was traditionally preformed just before going to war, which explains the strong beat and martial spirit, plus the swords they flash around in some of the dances. But now it is often performed at social gatherings like weddings and celebrations by both men and women.

☺ ☻ EXPLORATION: Arabian Desert

Watch a video about the Arabian Peninsula. We recommend *Wild Arabia* from the BBC. Then make this craft.

Use a coffee filter and bowls with saturated yellow and orange water, plus a dropper. Let the kids drip water slowly onto the coffee filter until it is completely covered with colored water. Let it dry. Glue to white paper. Then over the top place a silhouette frame cut out of black paper. You can use the camel template from the printables at the end of this unit if you'd like or you can make your own.

Fabulous Fact

The word *desert* originally meant "an abandoned place" and about 1/3 of the earth is considered desert land.

Writer's Workshop

Pick an animal that lives in the Arabian Desert and learn more about it. Write a report about what you've learned and share it with your family.

Here are some animals to consider:

gazelle

oryx

sand cat

spiny-tailed lizard

termites

dung beetle

dab lizard

SCIENCE: CLOUDS & PRECIPITATION

Fabulous Fact

Water droplets form around a "seed" of dust or bacteria in the air.

Clouds are where the water in the atmosphere gathers before falling back to Earth. The types of clouds you see in the sky can give you a pretty good idea of what the weather will be in a few hours or even the next day. Like everything else, people have named and classified clouds, though clouds, not caring, often form outside these "rules."

The three major types are cirrus, cumulus, and stratus into which the other cloud types have sub categories.

Here are the ten types of clouds:

Cloud Name	Appearance	Weather Associated with this type
Cirrus	High, long trails of clouds, sometimes called mare's tails	Wind high in the atmosphere will bring a change in the weather
Cirrostratus	Layer of thin, wispy clouds very high in the sky	Wet weather is on the way
Cirrocumulus	Heaped up high altitude clouds, can look like fish scales in the sky	Bring unpredictable changing weather
Altostratus	Slightly lower than cirrus clouds, form a thin gray veil across the sky	Rain is on the way
Altocumulus	High, small puffs of clouds, thickly scattered across the sky	Watch for thunderstorms
Stratocumulus	Form a heavy sheet of gray clouds across the sky, with a few gaps here and there for the sun to shine through	
Cumulus	Puffy white summer time clouds scattered across a blue sky	Good weather
Cumulonimbus clouds	Massive gray and black clouds that reach from low in the sky to billow thousands of feet high into huge towers	Definitely a storm
Stratus	Lowest clouds, they cover the sky completely and are sometimes fog	
Nimbostratus	Very low dark clouds that always bring rain or snow	Precipitation

Clouds are part of the water cycle. Another part is the precipitation that falls from the clouds, whether it's rain, snow, or hail. People, animals, and plants need water to survive and we get it from the clouds, all purified and salt free. Of course we complain if we get too much rain and we complain when we get too little.

☺ ☻ EXPLORATION: Cotton Ball Clouds

Re-create this picture of the types of clouds using cotton balls to create your own 3-D cloud diagram.

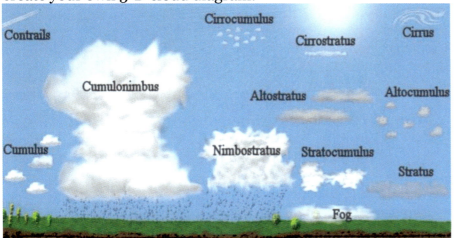

The thinner the cloud type is, the more you'll need to stretch out and manipulate the cotton balls. If you want gray cotton balls you can dye them ahead of time by putting some black food dye and water into a paper cup, soaking the cotton balls for a minute, and then spreading them on newspapers to let them dry.

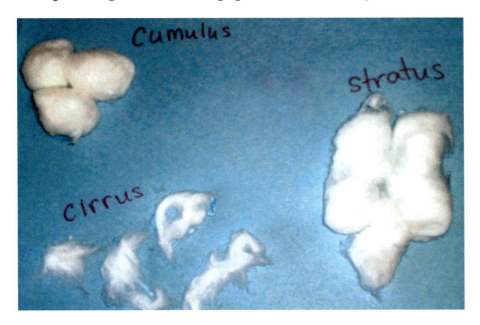

Additional Layer

Since the 1940's people have tried to change the weather through cloud seeding. Chemicals, usually either silver nitrate or frozen carbon dioxide (dry ice) are dropped into an existing cloud to make it precipitate out the rain it is carrying. Though the practice has been studied, tested and used for more than 80 years, no one knows if it really works.

Famous Folks

Luke Howard, a British chemist and amateur meteorologist came up with the naming system for clouds.

Deep Thoughts

If clouds are made of water, why do they float?

What would happen if a cloud suddenly crashed to the ground all at once? How much water is really in a cloud and how much does it weigh?

Why do clouds sometimes move the opposite direction from the wind?

On The Web

http://www.wildwildweather.com/precipitation.htm

Activities, experiments and information.

Additional Layer

If you've never laid out in a field of grass (or on your trampoline) in the summer time and watched the clouds with a friend, you should. Look for pictures in the sky and make up stories about them.

Once I even saw a flying saucer cloud right over a mountain. That kind of cloud is called a lenticular cloud.

😊 😃 EXPERIMENT: Cloud in a Bottle

To make your own cloud you need a clear two liter bottle, hot water, ice and a small dish.

1. Pour very hot water into the 2 liter bottle, until about 1/3 full.
2. Place a dish with ice cubes so it balances on the top of the bottle.

Water vapor will rise from the hot water and as it gets near the cold air from the ice cubes it condenses into larger droplets, forming a cloud.

😊 😃 EXPERIMENT: Rainmaker

You need a sauce pan, bowl, water and ice.

1. Bring 2 cups of water to a boil in a sauce pan.
2. Place at least six ice cubes in a bowl and hold over the steaming pot of water. Be careful not to burn yourself in the steam. An adult should hold the bowl.
3. Drops of water will form on the bottom of the bowl and as the drops run together and get more full, they drop back into the sauce pan.

This is basically what happens in the clouds. Water vapor gathers together, forming the cloud, because water molecules are more attracted to one another than to other molecules. Then as they get thicker and condense into droplets, they combine into bigger droplets until they fall from the sky as rain.

😊 😃 EXPLORATION: Rainy Day Painting

Make a rainy day painting. You need paint, paper, and cut outs from magazines or photos.

1. Thin blue or gray paint with water and spread liberally

along the top edge of a paper.

2. Hold the paper vertically so the paint drips down in long streamers.
3. Let it dry while you find some figures to add to the painting.
4. Cut out magazine pictures or your own photos of animals, people and objects that are getting caught in the rain.
5. Glue your cut outs onto your rainy picture.
6. Choose a light color like very light blue or white and drip that color over the photos.

Once it dries again you can paint in umbrellas and puddles if you wish.

☺ ☻ EXPLORATION: Foggy Day Painting

Make a foggy day painting. You will need paint, brushes, an old toothbrush and paper.

1. Paint a simple landscape with hills, a field, or a lake. In the foreground add a few trees and perhaps a building. If you live in a city, a city scape would work too. An ocean scene with a lighthouse would be another option. Any landscape at all will do!
2. Next, dab an old toothbrush in white paint and flick it all over your painting to create a foggy effect.

Additional Layer

How do you paint a cloud?

Beach View With Boats by Ary Pleysier

Drifting Clouds by Caspar David Friedrich (c. 1820)

Cloud Study by John Constable (1822)

The Pink Cloud by Paul Signac (1916)

Additional Layer

If you are lucky enough to live in a place with snow, then keep a record of the inches you get for at least one month. You need a large, straight sided container, like a bucket and a ruler. At the same time each day, go out and measure the inches or centimeters of snow you've received. Empty your bucket and let it accumulate for another day. Keep track of your data on a graph.

Additional Layer

Contrails are clouds formed in the wake of an airplane. They are made of water vapor like other clouds. The water vapor usually comes from the engines of the airplane, causing condensation.

Photograph by Joe Thomissen and shared under CC license.

☺ ☻ EXPLORATION: Precipitation

Water in clouds is frozen. Even in the summer time, the air at high altitudes is very cold. Except for sometimes in the tropics, the water in clouds is frozen water. As the drops fall they melt if they hit warmer air.

Draw a diagram to show what happens to form different types of precipitation.

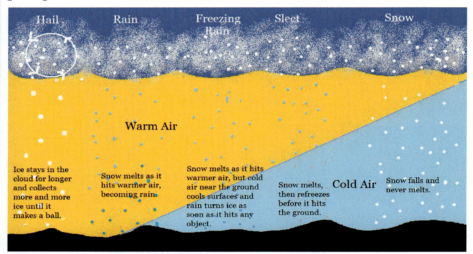

☺ ☺ ☻ EXPLORATION: Water Cycle

Start by looking at a glass of water. Can you guess how old this water is? We've been using the same old water since the beginning of the earth! The earth has a limited amount of water that just keeps going around and around, and that's why we call its movement "the water cycle."

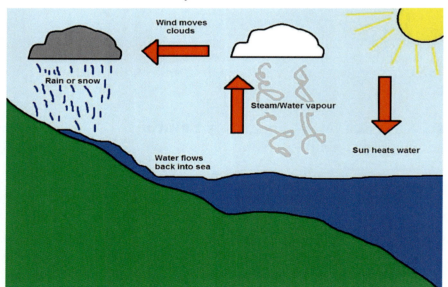

A very simplified version of the water cycle for young children.

Here are the basic parts of the water cycle:

1. **Evaporation** and **transpiration** – This is when the sun heats up the water so much that it turns into vapor and rises up from the lakes, oceans, and rivers and floats up into the air. Transpiration is the same process, except in this case it's plants that are losing their water to the sun's heat instead of a body of water.
2. **Condensation** – Water vapor up in the sky all gathers together as it cools. That's how we get clouds.
3. **Precipitation** – This is any kind of water that is falling on us from the clouds - rain, snow, hail, or sleet. The clouds eventually become so heavy that the air just can't hold the water that has condensed.
4. **Collection** – Once all that precipitation has come down it has to go somewhere! Some of it will end up going straight to the oceans or other bodies of water. Some will fall on the land, soak into the earth, and become ground water.

Next, the cycle begins all over again . . . and again . . . and again . .

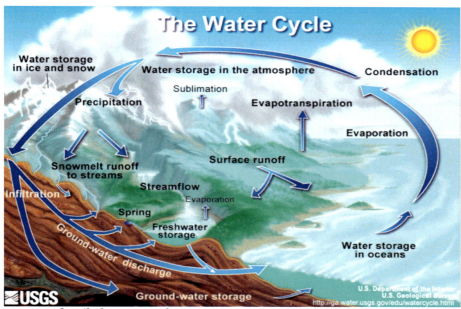

A more detailed water cycle representation courtesy of the U.S. Geological Survey

Make a poster of the water cycle. You can make it simple or complex depending upon the ages of the kids.

Have the kids draw a diagram of the water cycle. You can include water evaporating from oceans, lakes, the ground and so on. Also include clouds and rain and snow. Another important part of the

---

Additional Layer
Pour a glass of cold water on a hot day and set it outside. Over time you'll see water form on the glass. It didn't leak out of your cup. Nope! It came from the water vapor in the air, and turned to a liquid when it touched your cold glass.

On The Web
You can find lots of cool videos describing the water cycle, like this one from NASA:

http://youtu.be/o_coZz ZfC8c

Additional Layer
Acid rain occurs when gases, sulfur oxides and nitrogen oxide, dissolve in water in the air. This makes the water more acidic than usual. When the acid rain falls it can kill trees, fish, and other organisms, pit stone statues and buildings, and eat away steel structures like bridges.

Most pollutants are from coal burning power plants and automobiles. When the sulfur oxide is removed from plant emissions before being released in the air the problem disappears.

Additional Layer

How much more volume does snow take up than water? Collect snow in a straight sided, round or square dish. Measure the height of the snow, and the sides of the dish, and find the volume by multiplying the length and width (of the dish) and height (of the snow). Bring it inside and let it melt. Measure the height of the water in the dish and calculate the volume again. What is the difference? Can you calculate the percentage or fractional difference?

Fabulous Fact

The water cycle actually cools the earth. When water evaporates it absorbs heat. (That's why your body cools itself by sweating). Evaporative cooling reduces Earth's temperature by an estimated 52°C (94°F). That's a huge difference!

Fabulous Fact

The wettest place on Earth is Kauai, Hawaii. It is known as the garden isle and receives rain 350 days a year for an average annual rainfall of 460 inches.

water cycle that we don't think about too much is the ground water. When water passes through the earth it is purified and clean for people and animals to drink.

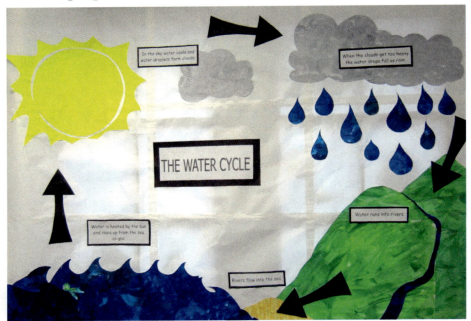

Even though water evaporates from land sources, by far the greatest amount of water vapor comes from the oceans. How does this explain dry or arid areas? Very wet areas?

☺ ☻ EXPERIMENT: Why Isn't Rain Salty?

Evaporation is an important part of the water cycle. If the ground water and water from the oceans didn't evaporate, we wouldn't ever get any more rain. The water would stay at the surface and never become clouds. If we get so much of our water from the ocean, why isn't rain salty? Do this little experiment to find out:

First, fill two mason jars about halfway with water. Stir a few tablespoons of salt into one of them (just enough that it pretty much all dissolves). Now set both of the jars out in the sunshine for a few days (hot weather works best). Watch what happens to each jar.

Where did the water go? What is left behind? Now can you answer the question about why rain isn't salty?

☺ ☻ ☻ EXPERIMENT: Colliding Air

You'll need: 2 clean, empty, identical baby food jars, an index card, red and blue dye, and water.

Pour hot tap water into a small glass jar to the top of the rim. Add

5 drops of red food coloring; stir. Fill the other jar with cold water and add 5 drops of blue food coloring; stir. Now cover the red jar with an index card or several layers of folded wax paper and hold it very tightly while you invert it and place it directly over the cold jar. Carefully remove the index card. Once it is removed, press the lips of the jars tightly together and gently turn them on their sides.

How do the two fronts travel in relation to one another? (This will make a mess. Do it over a bowl or the sink.)

Memorization Station

Memorize the major types of clouds. Practice identifying them in the sky as you drive around town or each morning as you check your weather station.

The same thing happens in nature. Hot water, like the hot air of a hot air balloon, rises. Hot is less dense than cold because its molecules are racing around quickly and staying farther apart. In weather, this means that when a cold front moves in, the warm air rushes upward and out of there!

On the Web

http://ga.water.usgs.gov/edu/watercycleprecipitation.html

Lots to learn. Plus you're paying for it, so use it.

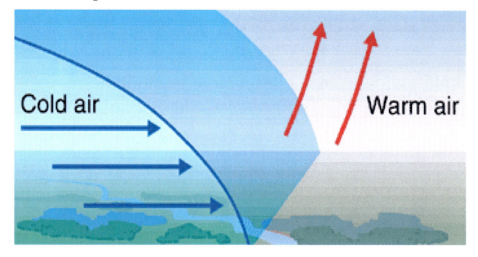

☺ ☺ ☺ **EXPERIMENT: Fronts**
Make a blue ice cube by freezing water that you have dyed blue with a few drops of food coloring. Fill a container 2/3 full with warm water. Now place the blue ice cube at one end of the warm-water container. At the other end, add 3 drops of red food coloring.

Additional Layer

Some places in the world get lots of snow, some places get none, and some places get somewhere in between. Discuss climate and weather patterns with your kids. See if they can figure out why Hawaii doesn't get snow, but Prince Edward Island, Canada gets lots. How much difference does the amount of sunlight make to a place on Earth?

The blue ice cube represents a pocket of cold air. The red water represents warm air. See how the air masses of warm and cold fronts cause movement in the air when they meet?

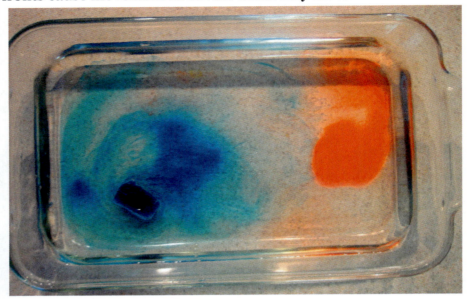

☺ ☺ ☺ EXPERIMENT: Making Air Pressure

Put a ping pong ball inside of a funnel and put the funnel into your mouth. Tilt your head back so the funnel is pointed straight up. Try to blow the ping pong ball out of the funnel.

What happened? Well, the air that you blew traveled around the edges of the ping pong ball, so it didn't push it straight up! You just created the same lift that airplanes use to fly, and the same air pressure you find in weather fronts.

EXPERIMENT: Blowing Paper and Bernoulli

Hold a piece of paper with two hands up by your mouth, letting the paper sag under it's own weight. Ask your kids what will happen when you blow on the top of the paper. They will likely expect the paper to be forced downward, but just the opposite will happen. Blow across the top of the paper gently and you will see the sheet of paper begin to lift up.

This happens because of lift. Bernoulli's Principle says that pressure is reduced where air is moving quickly. The pressure on the paper is actually reduced above the paper because of the moving air your breath provided; this is called lift. Airplanes fly because of lift. The moving plane starts a vortex of air circulating round the wing. The vortex

Additional Layer

If you could create a perfectly steady flow of air (like have a big balloon that is deflating very slowly into the mouth of the funnel), you should be able to tip the funnel upside down and the ping pong ball will still stay inside because of the lift you are creating just from air pressure.

Additional Layer

Hexagons are geometrical patterns and the hexagons in snowflakes are regular and symmetrical. Discuss some of the properties of hexagons – the number of sides and angles, the difference between a regular and irregular hexagon, and how a regular hexagon can be divided into fractions.

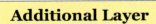

Additional Layer

Weather lore: "Red sky at night, sailor's delight." This old saying is true. Dust particles that make the sky look red indicate anticyclone, which brings fair weather.

combines with the general flow of air past the plane so that the combined flow pattern leads to faster air above the wing and hence less pressure above the wing. The higher pressure below the wing then creates lift and the plane goes up, up, and away.

☺ ● EXPLORATION: Snowflakes

Snowflakes are made up very high in the atmosphere. Way up there in the clouds, water is vapor, not even drops. It's so tiny that until several molecules can get together, the water can't even freeze into flakes. To get together, the water needs a nucleus or a particle around which it can form, usually dust particles in the air.

When conditions are very cold, we say the snow is dry. The flakes are usually very small, single crystals that come down by themselves and because they are so cold, do not melt and stick together. When the temperature is closer to freezing, then the crystals often stick together to make bigger flakes and are very packable for building snowmen and forts.

Make paper snowflakes. Just fold square sheets of paper and cut out triangles, circles, squares, and other more intricate shapes out of the edges. Unfold them to see the magical shapes you've created.

In nature snowflakes always have six sides, either simple hexagons or intricate branches, depending on conditions. Ice always forms into hexagonal crystals, because the molecular structure of water gives rise to this shape. But in spite of this basic similarity, every snowflake is unique. When you think of the trillions upon trillions that fall in just one snowstorm this is pretty amazing.

☺ ● EXPLORATION: Snow Globe
Make your own little snow globe. Start with a clean jar. Baby

Fabulous Fact
The world's tallest snowman, or woman as the case may be, was built in Bethel, Maine in 2008 and named after the governor, Olympia Snowe. Her eyelashes are made of skis.

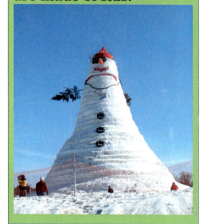

Famous Folks
The first person to discover the shape and uniqueness of snowflakes was a man named Wilson Bentley, who loved snow so much that when he grew up he made it his life's work. Read more about him in Snowflake Bentley by Jaquelin Briggs Martin. Visit this site to see some of his photographs of snowflakes. SnowflakeBently.com

Additional Layer

Snowflakes are classified into categories too: plate, column, star, dendrite, and capped column.

food jars or other small, clear jars work well. You can even use a plastic one if you are concerned about it breaking. Inside the jar you need to create a scene.

First, sand the inside of the lid a bit, then stick your pieces down using clear silicone, found in a hardware store. Use white sculpy clay stuck on to the inside of the jar's lid as your snow. Follow the baking instructions if you use sculpy. You can also use sculpy to make snowmen or other figurines, or you can purchase small figurines from the cake topper or toy section at the store. I can often find small figurines at the dollar store.

Once your scene is secure on the jar lid, fill the jar up almost to the top with distilled water. Add a small pinch of white or silver large particle glitter. Use an eye dropper to add a drop or two of glycerin. Get glycerin at the drug store. It will keep the glitter from falling too quickly.

Now you're done! Screw on the lid really tightly and give your snow globe a try!

THE ARTS: CREATIVE KIDS

This unit is different than every other art unit. Rather than focusing on historical art appreciation, principles of art, artists, and skills, the emphasis here is on creativity. So much of what we teach is directed. We ask kids to imitate what we are doing; this is a great way to learn things, but it doesn't teach original thought or creativity. In one unit of each year, we'll ask kids to become songwriters, inventors, and artists in their own right. This same unit will appear during one unit in each of the four years, with slightly different ideas to get you started. Each time your kids' projects should be new, unique, and completely decided upon by the child. Here are some creativity boosters to choose from:

☺ ☺ ☺ **EXPLORATION: Sell It To Me**
Your job is to create a commercial. You can use a real product or create your own new product. Write your script, complete with stage directions. Consider things like costumes, background music, and your scenery. Get some friends to help act in the commercial with you. You'll also need a camera man. Tape the commercial.

☺ ☺ ☺ **EXPLORATION: Children's Book**
Write and illustrate a children's book. It could be anything from an ABC book to a choose-your-own-adventure. Take a look at some of your favorite picture books for some ideas, and then get writing.

☺ ☺ ☺ **EXPLORATION: Puppeteer**
Write your own puppet show. Create your own story, or take an old story and write it with a new twist. You might change the

Explanation
Inventions don't have to be realistic when creativity is the goal. I once saw an invention I really wish I had thought of first. It was a pull-down shade with a customizable picture of a kid's bedroom, spic and span spotless. The idea was to mount it above the bedroom doorway and be able to pull down the shade over the entire doorway so your mom would look over and see a clean room no matter what the condition of the bedroom was behind the shade. Brilliant. Would it actually work? No. I'm a mother and I can promise it wouldn't work, but it's creative!

Karen

Writer's Workshop
Dialogue is very difficult for most people to write so it doesn't sound like a script. Listen carefully to the way real people talk in real conversations. What are their mannerisms and expressions?

Writer's Workshop

When you write a script for a puppet show or a story always start with a basic outline of major events that will happen. It also helps to keep track of your characters and their personalities on a separate sheet of paper, especially if there are more than two or three.

characters, the setting, or the time period. Along with the script, you'll need to create puppets. These could be paper bag puppets, sock puppets, stick puppets, some that you sew, or you could make marionettes. You may need to recruit helpers.

Practice your show and perform it for an audience.

☺ ☺ ☺ EXPLORATION: Be An Imagineer

Design your own amusement park ride. It could be simple ride like a new roller coaster, or a full attraction ride like the Imagineers at Disney design. At Disney they say, "If you can dream it, you can build it." Don't be inhibited by what's already out there. Begin by thinking of your favorite book or movie, then create a plan for the perfect ride centered around it.

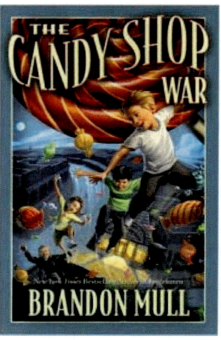

I love *The Candy Shop War* by Brandon Mull. I can already imagine the thrill of a ride along its themes of magical candy that gives you all kinds of powers, witches, searching for mysterious potion ingredients, and flying.

☺ ☺ ☺ EXPLORATION: Sewing and Fashion Design

If you like to sew, try designing an original look. Sketch a simple design. Head to the fabric store. Sew your look using a sewing machine. You don't need to use a pattern for this. Just create your own. If you'd like to you can tailor it to fit one of your dolls or stuffed animals.

If you're not really into fashion but would still like to sew, you can create some other useful item for one of your toys. My son sewed a sleeping bag for his stuffed frog and a quiver to hold arrows for himself. My daughters also like to design and sew their own purses and bags.

☺ ☺ ☺ EXPLORATION: Invention Convention

Create your own new invention. What would make life easier or better?

Begin by making a sketch of your invention. Diagram and describe its parts and functions. Write a description of how it will work. If possible, build a model or prototype of the invention. Name your invention and prepare a marketing plan. How much will it cost to build? How much will you sell it for? Where could you purchase it? Present your invention to an audience and describe it; convince them they need one!

☺ ☻ ☻ EXPLORATION: Dance To The Music

You'll need to start with a recording of a song you really like. When you're choosing your music, consider the genre, speed, and overall feel of the dance you'd like to create. You can include just yourself, or get some friends or siblings to join in with you. You might want to check out a variety of dancing styles from around the globe to get some fresh inspiration. (You Tube is a great place for this.)

Elizabeth, dancing to the Nutcracker Suite

Choreograph an original dance to the song. Consider your costume, lighting, and any background/stage/prop elements you may need. Practice the dance to perfection, then perform it for an audience.

☺ ☻ ☻ EXPLORATION: Third Time's A Charm

Look through your art portfolio or sketchbook and choose a piece of artwork. Now make three different versions of it. For example, if you made a watercolor painting, you might make a 3-D version of it with scrap wood, screws, and paint. You might do a detailed chalk sidewalk drawing. You could make it into pillowcase or skirt. You could turn it into a mosaic, a pointillism drawing, or a collage. Whatever you choose, make three very different versions of the same piece.

☺ ☻ ☻ EXPLORATION: Sing Me A Song

Using either your voice or an instrument, write an original song. Write it down, practice it, and plan a performance among your family or peers. For more musically advanced students, you can download Finale Notepad, music notation software, to create printed sheet music. It's inexpensive and really easy to use. You can find it at finalemusic.com.

Additional Layer

Besides being very creative, dance is also great exercise. A three-hour ballet performance is roughly equivalent to two 90-minute soccer games back to back or running 18 miles. And no worries if ballet isn't your cup of tea. There are too many styles of dance to even count, and no one is keeping you from making up your own style either.

On The Web

Check out www.creativitypool.com for some cool invention ideas. It's a categorized list of ideas people have for cool inventions. If people actually invent any of the items, the idea supplier gets credit and a reward. Submit your own ideas or you can use someone else's idea and actually invent it!

Teaching Tip

Sometimes we look at successful people and think they were just born talented. The truth is more prosaic. Hard work and practice. Kids can be easily frustrated if the vision in their minds isn't what they produce. Create a culture of practice, determination, and try-it-again in your house by practicing it yourself.

Teaching Tip

Creativity is the use of imagination or original thought. It's a hard thing to teach, because the only way to learn it is to keep trying and feel uninhibited in your efforts. Most young kids are naturally creative, but lose their imaginations the older they get. Unfortunately, creativity is much too easy to stifle, when we require precise things and regurgitation of information.

The son of a friend of mine once came home with a giant red "F" at the top of his coloring sheet. He had colored his elephant purple instead of gray. I wanted to scream at that teacher! We want kids who think outside the box, who think for themselves. Handing out F's for purple elephants is exactly how NOT to help creativity flourish.

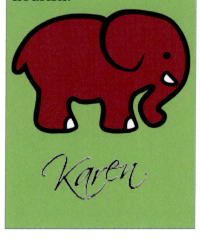

Karen

☺ ☻ ☺ **EXPLORATION: Chef in Training**

Create a meal that suits your taste. You can look through recipe books for ideas if you'd like, but don't just re-create what they've done. Add or change some of the ingredients. You may want to think about the design of the dish along with the taste. Sometimes the look of the dish can be as exciting as the flavor. Name your dish and be prepared to describe it. You may want to prepare several side dishes to accompany your creation. Your dish may be more on the fun, creative side, or it could be more traditional, but whatever you make, make it a work of art.

Arrange a dinner to serve your new dish at. Set a beautiful table – consider dishes, place mats, place cards, and centerpieces.

☺ ☻ ☺ **EXPLORATION: 10 Ingredient Free Art**

For this exploration, you can make anything you want! You are limited only by your supplies. Select 10 random art supplies out of a sack. Make an art piece that uses all ten things.

Here's a list of supplies to consider:
- paper (lots of kinds to choose from)
- pencil
- markers
- colored pencils
- chalks
- crayons
- oil pastels
- glue (lots of kinds to choose from)
- tape
- paints (choose from tempera, watercolor, finger paints, oil paints, acrylics)
- paintbrushes
- pom poms
- foam shapes
- stickers
- pipe cleaners

- wiggly eyes
- glitter
- cotton balls
- wood
- egg cartons
- cardboard
- tissue paper
- toilet paper/ paper towel rolls
- clay
- paper plates and cups
- feathers
- yarn
- fabric
- wire
- milk cartons or other empty food packaging
- straws
- foil, plastic wrap, waxed paper
- balloons
- small household items (marbles, tiles, picture frames, dishes, etc.)
- natural items (leaves, shells, stones, bark, dirt, etc.)
- food items (beans, rice, sugar, pasta noodles, dry dog food, etc.)

EXPLORATION: Speed Art

Create 25 pictures in your sketchbook in an hour's time. You'll have to work quickly. Just sketch whatever comes to mind. Let one idea run into the next, and then the next, and then the next. It's like that word association game where I say "baby" and you immediately reply "diaper." Take the first sketch and connect it with the second one, like a train. Then let that sketch connect to the following one. Continue on for the whole hour. Then go back and describe your thought process to someone as you show your sketches.

Teaching Tip
Don't be constrained by the traditional uses of art supplies. White glue makes beautiful 3-D paint when combined with tempera paint. What else can you use in new ways?

Explanation
Although young kids are creatively uninhibited, they are usually stranger inhibited. They won't always be willing to show off creativity to others because of their discomfort around strangers.

Teaching Tip
A trip to your pantry, yard, or the thrift store can easily provide unconventional art supplies.

Coming up next . . .

Unit 2-4

Vikings – Norway
Special Effects
Viking Art

My Ideas For This Unit:

Title: _____   Topic: _____

_____

_____

_____

_____

_____

_____

_____

_____

Title: _____   Topic: _____

_____

_____

_____

_____

_____

_____

_____

_____

Title: _____   Topic: _____

_____

_____

_____

_____

_____

_____

_____

_____

My Ideas For This Unit:

Title: _____ Topic: _____

_____

_____

_____

_____

_____

_____

_____

_____

Title: _____ Topic: _____

_____

_____

_____

_____

_____

_____

_____

_____

_____

_____

Title: _____ Topic: _____

_____

_____

_____

_____

_____

_____

_____

_____

_____

Symbols of Islam

The crescent moon and star are an old symbol of Islam. In fact, many scholars believe they pre-date Islam and were used by Arab tribes before the Prophet Mohammed ever lived. The color green is also a common symbol of Islam and Islamic nations.

Islam: Unit 2-3

610 AD 2-3

Mohammed receives first vision

610-622 AD 2-3

Mohammed preaches in Mecca

622 AD 2-3

Hejira, when Mohammed flees Mecca (start of Islamic calendar)

630 AD 2-3

Muslims capture Mecca, Arabian tribes vow allegiance

632 AD 2-3

Mohammed dies and Abu Bakr is first Caliph

633 AD 2-3

Muslim conquests begin

650 AD 2-3

The Koran is written down for the first time

680 AD 2-3

Shi'a sect begins

732 AD 2-3

Muslim Empire reaches largest point

Mosque

Mohammed fled from Mecca with his friend, Abu Bakir. They hid in a cave for three days while men searched for him.

The End

Colored by: _____

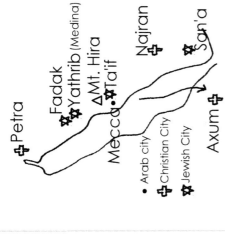

Some of Mohammed's followers heard there was a plot to assassinate him.

Petra
Fadak
Yathrib (Medina)
Mt. Hira
Mecca • Ta'if
Najran
San'a
Axum

• Arab city
✝ Christian City
✡ Jewish City

Mohammed had been preaching in Mecca, but a lot of people didn't like it. Some of his followers had already fled to Axum, a Christian kingdom across the sea.

The next Friday Mohammed went to Medina for prayers. He moved permanently to Medina where he united the tribes with a fair set of laws. He convinced them he was a prophet and had seen a vision.

The first thing Mohammed did when he got there was to lay the first stones for the very first Mosque at Quba, on the outskirts of the city.

The Hejira

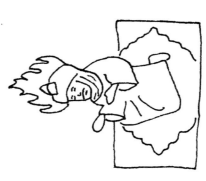

It took them ten more days to make their way north to the city of Medina.

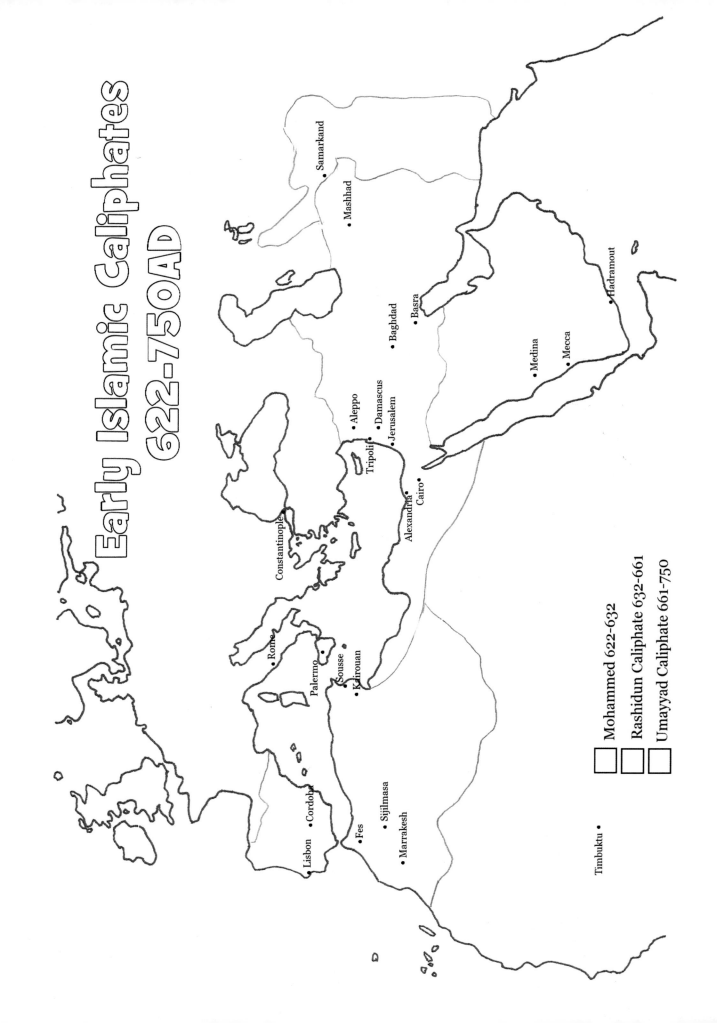

Early Islamic Caliphates
622-750AD

Samarkand

Mashhad

Hadramout

Baghdad

Basra

Medina

Mecca

Aleppo

Damascus

Jerusalem

Tripoli

Alexandria

Cairo

Constantinople

Rome

Palermo

Sousse

Kairouan

Lisbon

Cordoba

Fes

Sijilmasa

Marrakesh

Timbuktu

Mohammed 622-632

Rashidun Caliphate 632-661

Umayyad Caliphate 661-750

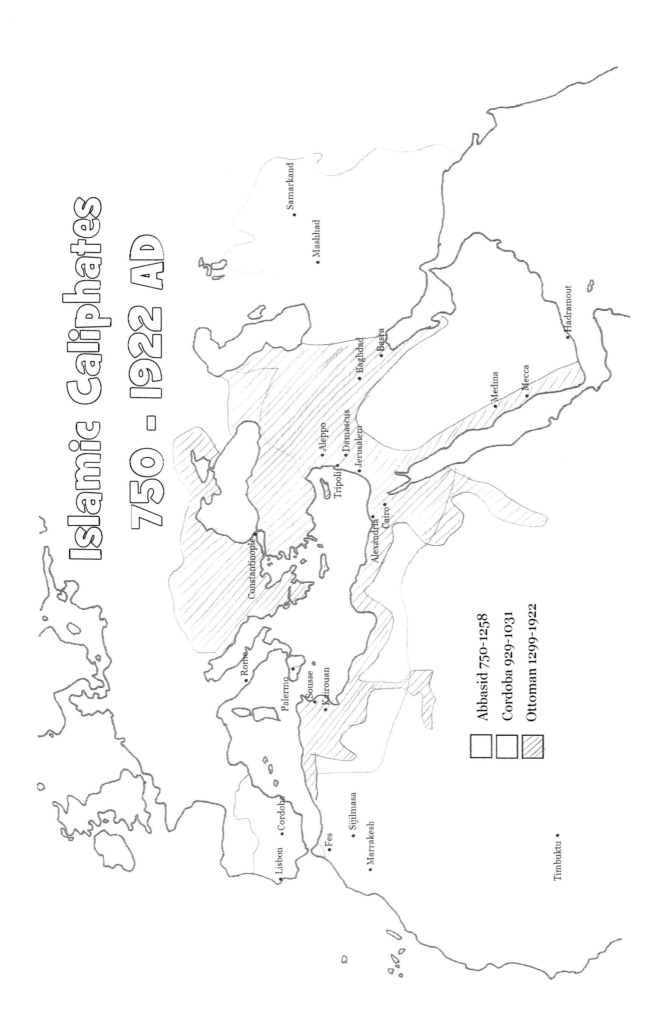

Islamic Caliphates
750 - 1922 AD

Samarkand

Mashhad

Hadramout

Basra

Baghdad

Medina

Mecca

Aleppo

Damascus

Jerusalem

Tripoli

Alexandria

Cairo

Constantinople

Rome

Palermo

Sousse

Kairouan

Lisbon

Cordoba

Fes

Sijilmasa

Marrakesh

Timbuktu

Abbasid 750-1258

Cordoba 929-1031

Ottoman 1299-1922

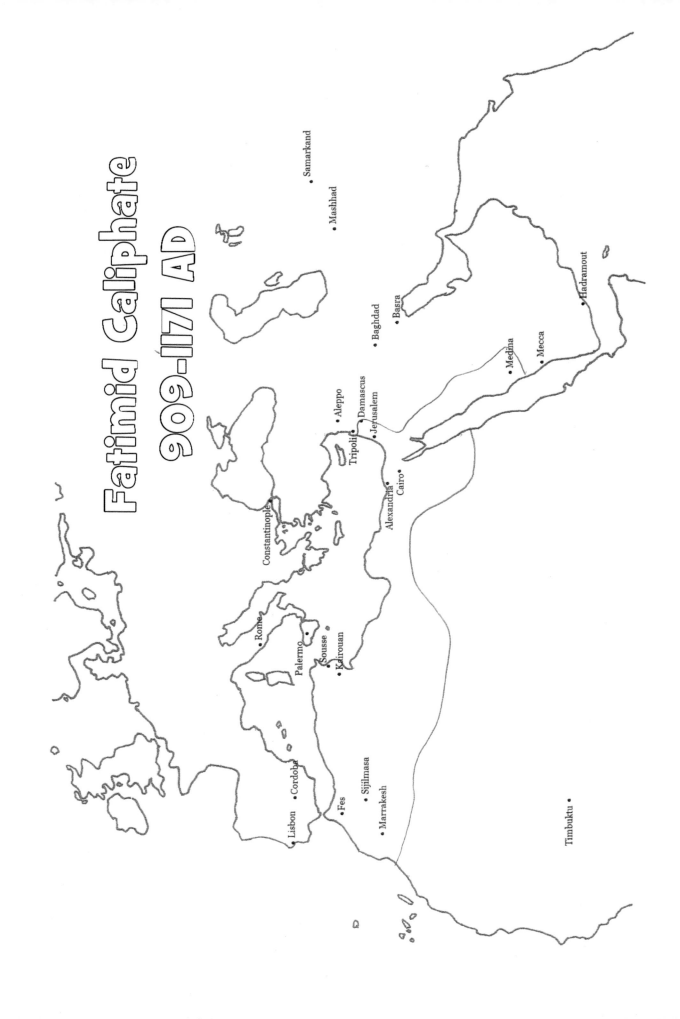

Fatimid Caliphate
909-1171 AD

Samarkand

Mashhad

Baghdad

Basra

Hadramout

Medina

Mecca

Aleppo

Damascus

Jerusalem

Tripoli

Alexandria

Cairo

Constantinople

Rome

Palermo

Sousse

Kairouan

Lisbon

Cordoba

Fes

Sijilmasa

Marrakesh

Timbuktu

The Five Pillars of Islam

Cut out each rectangle, decorate, and then glue into a cylinder.

shahada
There is no god but God and Mohammed is his prophet

salah
Prayer five times a day

zakat
Give alms to the poor

hajj
Pilgrimage to Mecca at least once

ramadan
Fast during the holy month

Arabian Peninsula

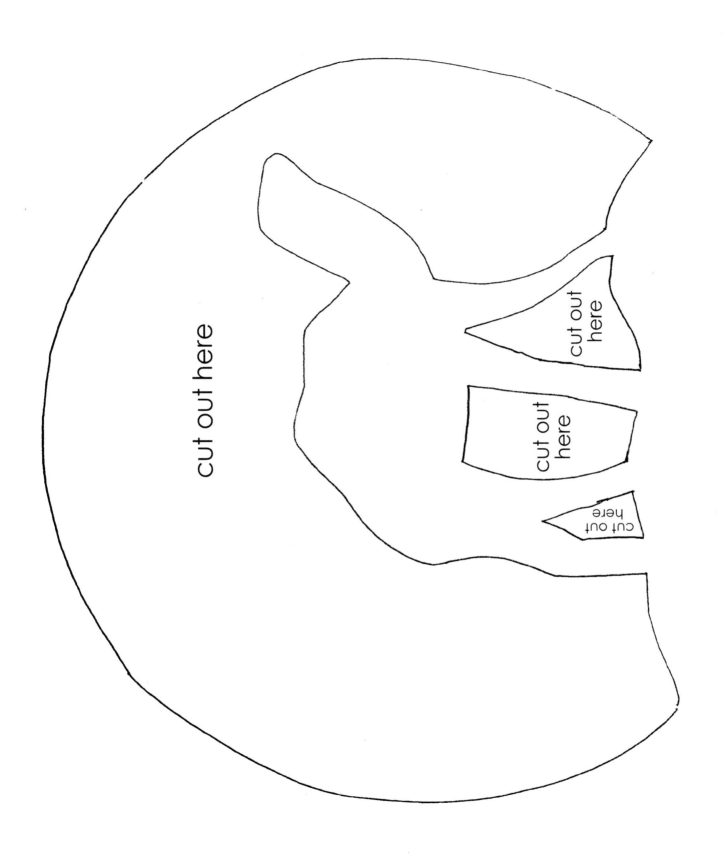

ABOUT THE AUTHORS

Karen & Michelle . . .
Mothers, sisters, teachers, women who are passionate
about educating kids.
We are dedicated to lifelong learning.

Karen, a mother of four, who has homeschooled her kids for more than eight years with her husband, Bob, has a bachelor's degree in child development with an emphasis in education. She lives in Utah where she gardens, teaches piano, and plays an excruciating number of board games with her kids. Karen is our resident Arts expert and English guru {most necessary as Michelle regularly and carelessly mangles the English language and occasionally steps over the bounds of polite society}.

Michelle and her husband, Cameron, homeschooling now for over a decade, teach their six boys on their ten acres in beautiful Idaho country. Michelle earned a bachelor's in biology, making her the resident Science expert, though she is mocked by her friends for being the *Botanist with the Black Thumb of Death*. She also is the go-to for History and Government. She believes in staying up late, hot chocolate, and a no whining policy. We both pitch in on Geography, in case you were wondering, and are on a continual quest for knowledge.

Visit our constantly updated blog for tons of free ideas,
free printables, and more cool stuff for sale:
www.Layers-of-Learning.com

Made in the USA
Middletown, DE
04 April 2025

73769537R00033